300

GAME

JOKES

THE ULTIMATE JOKE BOOK FOR KIDS AND TEENS (VOL 1 + 2)

Association and a Committee of Publishers and Associations.

contained within is the solitary and utter responsibility of the recipient reader. Under no circumstances will any legal responsibility or blame be held against the publisher for any reparation, damages, or monetary loss due to the information herein, either directly or indirectly.

Respective authors and companies own all copyrights not held by the publisher.

The information herein is offered for informational purposes solely and is universal as so. The presentation of the information is without a contract or any type of guarantee assurance.

Table of Contents

Nintendo Jokes

Q: What do you call a Pokemon that can't move very fast?

A: A Slow-poke

Q: What did Link use to win the basketball game?

A: His hookshot

Q: What do you get when you cross Sonic The Hedgehog and Curious George?

A: 2 Fast 2 Curious

Q: What is Sonic's favorite season?

A: Spring

Q: What happens if you tape an explosive to a hedgehog?

A: A Sonic Boom

Q: I asked my dad why he's playing Pokemon

A: He said Wyanaut.

Q: What does Sonic use to knock on doors?

A: His Knuckles

Q: What do you get when you cross Epona with a DeLorian

A: A Link to the past

Q: What does a gorilla wear to the beach?

A: Donkey Thong

Q: What is Samus's favorite food?

A: Metroid Prime Rib

Q: What does Princess Peach sit on at a bar?

A: A Toad Stool

Q: How does Yoshi feel after working out at the gym?

A: Dino-sore

Q: How does Donkey Kong react when he sees a boat?

A: He goes ape ship

Q: What is Zelda's favorite breakfast dish?

A: Eggs and sausage Link

Q: What is the Nintendo Wii called in France?

A: Nintendo Yes

Q: How come Toad gets invited to every party?

A: Because he's a fun-gi.

Q: What did Wario name his art store?

A: World of Wario Craft

Q: Why did Mario cross the road?

A: Because he couldn't find a warp pipe.

Q: What is Mario's favorite play?

A: Mamma Mia

Q: What did Luigi use to talk to boos?

A: A LOUIJI board

Q: Why are Koopa Troopas antisocial?

A: Because they live a shell-tered life.

Knock Knock

Who's there?

Luigi.

Luigi who?

Mario's unnoticed brother.

Q: How do you fit 100 Pikachus in a bus?

A: You Poke'em on.

Q: What does Mario use to help with his shopping?

A: A Mario cart

Q: Why did Mario go to Luigi's mansion?

A: Because he heard there was a pack of boos hidden somewhere.

Q: Why did Mario get a goldfish as a pet?

A: Because they were so cheep-cheep.

Q: Why is Bowser so mean?

A: Because he koopas (coupes up) his feelings.

Q: What's Mario's favorite pokemon?

A: Lucario!

Q: Why did Miyamoto flip over the table?

A: He was having a Wii fit!

Q: What advice did Zelda give to Link so he could break into her castle?

A: Tri-force.

Q: What did Paper Mario say to the rock?

A: I win.

Q: Which Nintendo character sucks?

A: Kirby

Q: What school did Link go to after middle school?

A: High-rule school

Q: What do you say when you lose at Wii?

A: I want a wii-match.

A PS4 got injured and the Xbox called the ambulance.

Wii U Wii U Wii U Wii U

Yo momma so fat even Kirby can't eat her!

Q: Why does Donkey Kong always brush his teeth?

A: To prevent tooth DK.

Q: Why does Donkey Kong eat bananas?

A: He finds them a-peeling.

Q: Why didn't Dry Bones cross the road?

A: Because he didn't have the guts.

Q: How did Sonic beat up Tails?

A: He used his Knuckles.

I was going to make a Nintendo joke but it was Wii too hard for Mii to think of one.

My wife left me because I bought a Nintendo. Guess it was time for a Switch.

My girlfriend told me to stop playing Pokemon as it was childish.

I started thrashing about and roared "You don't have enough badges to control me!"

Q: What is Mega Man's favorite drink?

A: Dr.Light

Minecraft Jokes

Q: Why are there no cars in Minecraft?

A: The roads are all blocked off.

Q: What's a ghast's favorite country?

A: The Nether-Lands

Q: What did the teacher say to the curious cat?

A: You Ocelot of questions.

Q: How do you cure hunger in Minecraft?

A: By eating three square meals.

Q: What do you call a Minecraft celebration?

A: A block party

Q: How does Steve cut down trees with his hands?

A: How wood I know!

Q: Why don't blazes ever make businesses?

A: They keep firing people.

Q: How does Steve get his exercise?

A: He runs around the block.

Q: Why did the creeper cross the road?

A: Because there was an ocelot chasing him.

Q: Hear about the creeper that went to the party?

A: He had a blast!

Q: Where does Steve rent movies?

A: Blockbuster

Q: Why did the mushroom make such a fun roommate?

A: Because he was such a fungi.

Q: How does Steve measure his shoe size?

A: In square feet

Q: What city do most wolves live in?

A: Howllywood, California

Q: Where do miners sleep?

A: On their bed rocks.

Q: What did the ocean say to the chicken?

A: Nothing. It just waved.

Q: How does Steve get his exercise?

A: By running around the block

Q: What do skeletons say before dining?

A: Bone appetit

Q: What is a creeper's favorite subject?

A: Hissssssssstory

Q: What time is it when six ocelots chase Steve?

A: Six after one

Q: Where do you shear sheep?

A: At the baa-baa shop

Q: What did Steve say to his girlfriend?

A: I dig you.

Q: Why can't you score against Minecraft basketball players?

A: They know how to block

Q: What is the name of Minecraft's boy band?

A: Kids on the Block

Q: Why did the creeper cross the road?

A: To get to the other sssssssside.

Q: What do you put on top of a creeper's ice cream sundae?

A: Whipped scream

Q: What is Cobblestone's favorite type of music?

A: Rock music

Q: Why are zombies so good at Minecraft?

A: Because of their DEADication.

Q: Why didn't the enderman cross the road?

A: Because he teleported.

Q: What is a creeper's favorite food?

A: Ssssssssssalad

Q: What kind of makeup do witches use?

A: Mas-scare-a

Q: Why didn't the skeleton go to the prom?

A: He had no body to dance with.

Q: What musical instruments do skeletons play with?

A: Trom-bone

Q: What is the national sport of Minecraft?

A: Boxing

Q: How good is Minecraft?

A: It's Top-Notch!

Q: Why did the sailor bring gold and silver on to the boat?

A: He needed ores (oars).

Q: Why do you always find zombies at Subway?

A: Because they like to "Eat Flesh".

Q: What did Steve say to the zombie?

A: You want a piece of me?

Q: Why couldn't the Zombie Pigman get out of the lava?

A: Because he was a slow-pork.

Q: Why did the hostile mob explode in the middle of the dance party?

A: They were just creeping it real.

Q: Where do most hostile mobs come from?

A: North and South Scarolina

Q: What do zombies and skeletons need in the morning?

A: SunBLOCK

Runescape Jokes

I saw someone killing red spiders a few years ago and reported him for bug abuse.

Your momma's so fat she's got enough chins for 99 range

Q: How many Runescape players does it take to change a lightbulb?

A: 50, 1 to change it and the rest to complain about how the old one was better.

Yo momma so fat she joined her own clan and it said clan full.

Yo momma so dumb she sold her bow for arrows.

Yo momma so fat she takes up her own inventory spaces.

Q: Why did the noob cross the road?

A: To get to the other guide.

Q: How hard is it to get a Champion's Scroll?

A: Pretty imp-possible

Q: Why did the noob cross the road?

A: Because he couldn't teleport.

DOTA 2 Jokes

Q: Do you know the shortest DOTA joke?

A: LoL

A LoL player and a Dota 2 player walk into a bar. The Dota 2 player tells the LoL player: Dota 2 is better. The LoL player couldn't deny.

Q: Why did Emberspirit get muted?

A: Because he's a flamer.

Q: Who did Faceless Void thank when he carried the game?

A: His MoM and DaeD

Q: What does Luna like on her sandwhiches?

A: Salad Mayonnaise

Q: Why did Kunkka go to Jail?

A: He torrents too much.

Q: Why does Luna hate Venomancer?

A: He always tries to Poison Nova.

Q: What is Tinker's favourite month?

A: march March MARCH!

Q: What did Pugna say at the rehab facility?

A: Let me take a crack addict (at it).

Q: Why is Pugna a bad support?

A: Cause he nether wards.

Q: Where does Spirit Breaker go toilet?

A: The Bara-thurum (bathroom)

Q: How do you know Dota 2 is a popular game?

A: 9/10 people play it.

Q: Why did Earthspirit fail gymnastics?

A: He could never be balanced.

Q: What did Tidehunter say to the comedian?

A: You're kraken me up.

Yo momma's so fat her passive aura is heart of tarrasque.

Yo momma's so fat it takes 5 Chens to heal her back to 100hp.

Yo momma's so fat pudge's hooks breaks.

Yo momma's so fat, she can push 3 lanes at once.

I better buy spell immunity because you are stunnin'.

Q: Who did Sladar send flowers to?

A: His Slihereen Crush

Q: Did you hear about Naga killing Tidehunter?

A: RIP Tide

Q: How did Chen know he was in love with Enchantress

A: Because the further he got from her the more it hurt.

So Newbee just banned Nature's Prophet and Death's Prophet. Guess you could say they are a non-prophet organization!

Q: Why did legion commander have to re-bind her keys?

A: Because she couldn't press the attack button.

Q: Why was Abaddon kicked out of the mafia?

A: He turned out to be a bad don.

Q: How does a carry ask a support to dance?

A: "Tango plz"

Q: How did the enemy know where Treant was hiding?

A: Because Timber saw.

Q: What is Witch Doctor's email address?

A: Look@it.go

Q: Why did Lich have to stop riding his bike?

A: His chain was frosted.

Q: When does Anti-Mage finish farming?

A: 3 AM

Q: Why is Anti-Mage enemies with everyone?

A: Because friendship is magic.

Q: Why doesn't Eminem play support?

A: Because he opens his mouth but the wards won't come out.

Q: What do you call a teamfight where Visage has no birds?

A: An unfamiliar situation.

Q: Why does Slardar hate Rubick?

A: Because he stole his crush.

Q: Why is Roshan depressed?

A: He's been in that pit for Aegis.

Q: Why did Huskar use his ultimate 3 times?

A: He wanted Half Life 3.

Q: Why is EG protecting Fear?

A: They have to defend the ancient.

Q: Why wasn't Clinkz at his prom?

A: He had nobody to go with.

Q: Why did Wraith King decide to buy Drums?What do you call an Ogre + Jakiro dual lane?

A: He wanted to join the Wraith Band.

I heard Bounty Hunter works as a musician in his spare time... and makes good money from his tracks.

Q: What do you call a Faceless Void with a Divine Rapier?

A: Avoid

Q: Why isn't Shadow Fiend a father?

A: No one wants to see him raze a child.

Q: Why is Riki's mom sad?

A: Because he disappeared when he hit 6.

Q: Why don't League players use Facebook?

A: Because they can't block creeps.

Q: Why is your brother bad at playing Rubick?

A: He can't Spell Steal.

Q: Who is the best support?

A: James Bond because he is 007.

Q: Why did Shadow Fiend buy 6 different boots?

A: He wanted more soles.

Enjoying the book so far? Let us know what you think by leaving a review!

What has been your favorite joke from the book?

Miscellaneous Jokes

Q: **Why are cats so good at video games?**

A: Because they have nine lives.

Q: **Why do they call it the PS4?**

A: There are only 4 games worth playing.

Q: **What does a guy with a bad hip and the PS4 have in common?**

A: They both have trouble getting back up.

Q: What does Lara eat for dinner?

A: Croft macaroni and cheese

Q: Why is a Jedi never lonely?

A: Because the Force is always with him.

Q: What do you call a friend that never lets you play?

A: A Kontrol Freek

Q: Why did Dante refuse to cut onions?

A: He was afraid that the Devil May Cry.

Q: Why did Sony hire Justin Timberlake after PSN went down?

A: They hoped he could bring Sexy Back.

Q: What's the difference between playing Pokemon Go and going to Comic Con?

A: At Comic Con, you can catch real ones.

Mario is red, Sonic is blue, press start to join and be my player 2.

How long before people start naming kids after Pokemon?

Video games ruined my life. Good things I have 3 lives left.

Don't be racist. Be like Mario. An Italian plumber, created by Japan, who speaks English.

Video games don't make me violent and angry. Lag does.

My friend told me he didn't have much to drink last night even though he gave me a mushroom and said "Grow Mario grow!"

Fortnite Jokes

Q: What game mode do cows play?

A: Cattle Royale

Q: Who does the Floss at Buckingham Palace?

A: The Royale Family

Q: Why aren't skeletons any good at Fortnite?

A: They have no skins!

Q: How can you make your TV dance?

A: By using the emote control!

Q: How come ball hogs aren't good at Fortnite?

A: They don't battle pass.

Q: What's the similarity between X-Men and Fortnite?

A: They both have an OP Storm.

Q: Why do Fortnite players have nice teeth?

A: Because they Floss.

Q: Did you hear about the thieves that broke into the factory?

A: Heard they took an L.

Q: How long did it take you to come up with that joke?

A: About a fortnight

Q: What do you think of my jokes?

A: You really need to bush up on your jokes.

A: They HAUNTED me. You should probably go back to your RETAIL job.

Q: Where would a poor person land in Fortnite?

A: Peasant Park

How tough am I? I play Fortnite.

Yeah so?

And only drop at Tilted Towers.

Right this way sir.

Me jumping out at an enemy
running past the bush I'm hiding in

Yo mama's so fat, her glider in Fortnite is a jumbo jet.

Yo mama's so fat, a Chug Jug only restores a quarter of her HP.

Yo mama's so ugly, even the bus driver jumped out.

Yo mama's so fat that her skin takes up all the slots on Fortnite.

Yo mama's so fat, we thought she was the one that turned Dusty Depot to Dusty Divot.

Yo mama's so ugly that the bus driver thanked her for jumping out.

Yo mama's so fat she was already in the Storm at the start of the game.

Yo mama's so short, she drowned in Loot Lake.

League of Legends Jokes

Q: Why is Master Yi's Q so buggy?

A: Because it's "Alpha" Strike.

Q: What car does Garen drive?

A: A ForD Emacia

Q: What's the number one religion in LoL?

A: Siontology

Q: How do you take care of a toxic Zyra?

A: Repot them!

Q: What do you call a Warwick that's MIA?

A: A wherewolf

Q: What do you call a Renekton wearing a vest?

A: An in-vest-i-gator

Q: What do Malphite and Rammus listen to?

A: Rock 'n' Roll

Q: Why is Zilean the master of clocks?

A: He has a Zilean clocks.

Q: Why can't Gangplank play cards?

A: He's always on the deck.

Q: How long does it take to save up for a Locket?

A: Aegis

Q: What do you call an AFK Shyvana?

A: A Statikk Shyv

Q: What is a marksman's favorite vegetable?

A: A-kali flower

Q: Did you know Alistar is dyslexic?

A: He always goes oom.

Q: Why is Nautilus so good at killing people under towers?

A: Because he wears a diving suit.

Q: Who does Yorick have a crush on?

A: I hear he really digs Graves.

Q: Why does Teemo live in small house?

A: He doesn't need mushroom.

Q: Why did Twisted Fate get deported?

A: He didn't have a green card.

Q: Why did Syndra run away when she went oom?

A: She didn't have the balls to keep fighting.

Q: What do you call a game winning laser?

A: Viktor-e

Q: Did you hear about what happened to Singed's Twitter followers?

A: They died because he was too toxic.

Q: How does Janna shield her allies?

A: With ease (E's)

Q: What do you call a cross-dressing Zilean?

A: A Brazillian

Q: What is Lee Sin's favorite game mode?

A: Blind pick

Q: What's Vayne's favorite website?

A: Tumblr

Yo mama's so fat that when she recalled, all 3 lanes pinged MIA.

Q: Why does Taliyah love bread?

A: Because she's a sand witch.

Q: Did you hear what happened when Blitz went on a date with Orianna?

A: He knocked her up.

Q: How does Sona charge her phone?

A: With a Power Chord

Q: Why did Sivir lose the Spelling Bee?

A: She could only Spell Shield.

Lee Sin walks into a bar.

And a table. And a chair.

Q: Why can't Olaf park in a handicap spot?

A: Because he can't be disabled.

Q: Why did Zyra get banned?

A: She had too many leaves.

Q: Why are garbage men so good at League?

A: They're used to carrying trash.

Q: How many Bronze players does it take to change the lightbulb?

A: It's impossible. They can't even climb the ladder.

Q: Why does Fizz always fall off his pole?

A: He's unbalanced.

Q: What do you call a Fizz in stasis?

A: A goldfish

Q: Why does Soraka throw bananas?

A: She can't peel.

Yo mama's so fat that Rocket Grab turned into Bandage Toss.

Q: Why did Brand get banned?

A: He was flaming.

Q: Why do chefs love cooking for Ekko?

A: He always goes back 4 seconds.

Q: Why was Jinx pulled over on the highway?

A: She was going AD over.

Q: Why is Yasuo a good teammate?

A: He always hasakey!

World of Warcraft Jokes

Q: What do you call a Tauren Rogue?

A: Invisibull

Q: How does a Druid cut his hair?

A: Eclipse it.

Q: How hard is it to get a Champion's Scroll?

A: Pretty imp-possible

Q: How did the Paladin start losing weight?

A: He started eating light.

Q: Why didn't the Undead cross the road?

A: He didn't have the guts.

Q: Why wasn't the dragon invited to the party?

A: Because he was dragon everyone down.

Q: Why did the raid wipe on Terrace?

A: Because they took tsulong to kill the boss.

Q: Where does Ragnaros go for his back treatments?

A: The pyro-practor

Q: Why do hardcore raiders smell?

A: Because they never wipe.

Q: Why did the enchanter have to clean his bank?

A: It was full of dust.

Yo mama's so fat, she's exalted with McDonalds.

Q: Why are Warriors the worst salesmen?

A: They charge too much!

Yo mama's so fat, when a Rogue shadowstepped her, he got a loading screen.

Yo mama's so fat, when a Mage polymorphed her, she turned into a whale.

Yo mama's so fat that when she logged into WoW for the first time, she brought about the Cataclysm.

Yo mama's so fat that all her gear is "of the Whale".

Yo mama's so fat that when she casts Frost Nova, she causes an ice age.

Q: When a Tauren sees lightning but hears nothing, what does he call it?

A: A Thunder Bluff

Q: Why didn't the Warrior cross the road?

A: No path available

Q: What do you call a Druid who melees in tree form?

A: A combat log

Q: What do you get if you cross a Gnome and a Tauren?

A: A mini-taur

Q: Why are mages considered so polite?

A: They have a lot of Manas.

Q: What's the abbreviation for a Death Knight?

A: Decay

Q: What would you call Chromie's hips?

A: A waist of time

Overwatch Jokes

Take it from McCree and Reaper, these jokes Mei blow your mind.

Q: Why is Mercy the best support?

A: Because she has high heals!

Q: What was Roadhog's favorite activity?

A: He liked to hit the ice and play hooky.

Q: What's Mei's favorite dance?

A: She likes it when you watch her whip then watch her Mei Mei.

Q: Why is Junkrat such a likeable guy?

A: He has such an explosive personality.

Q: What did Pharah say when it was hailing?

A: Just ice rains from above.

Q: What did Zenyatta say when Tracer asked if something was in his eye?

A: Yes it's in the iris.

Q: Why is Torbjörn the most under appreciated defense character?

A: He has trouble standing up to the rest.

Q: Why is Roadhog such a likeable guy?

A: I don't know but I'm always hooked after talking to him.

Q: How did McCree do in the beauty pageant?

A: He was stunning.

Q: Why is Junkrat such a handful?

A: He always leaves everyone tired.

Q: What is Reaper's day job?

A: He is the repo-man.

Q: Why is Lúcio not aloud in the produce section?

A: He's always dropping beats.

Q: What's Reaper's favorite bread?

A: RYE! RYE! RYE!

Q: Why can't Reaper stop dancing?

A: Because his hips don't LIE LIE LIE!

Q: Does Torbjörn have a crush on Mei?

A: Yeah but she keeps giving him the cold shoulder.

Q: Have you ever been on Widowmaker's webpage?

A: I heard it's impossible to escape her site.

The Play of the Game showed Reinhardt using his Ultimate to get a multi-kill. The other team didn't find it too funny, but the ground was cracking up!

Yo mama's so fat that Roadhog ended up being pulled instead.

Yo mama's so fat that McCree got his ultimate on her 6 times.

Yo mama's so fat that Soldier 76's ultimate is useless.

Q: Why did Lucio fail his construction project?

A: He kept breaking it down.

Q: Why do all the ladies love Winston?

A: Because of his shocking personality.

Q: Why does Reaper want to be a pilot?

A: He wants to FLY FLY FLY!

Q: Who is Reinhardt's favorite music artist?

A: Mc Hammer

Q: What plastic surgery did they have to do on Reinhardt?

A: Rein-o-plasty

Q: Why did Reinhardt close up shop early?

A: There was no one left to charge.

Q: What's Reinhardt's favorite animal?

A: Rein-os.

Q: What's Reinhardt's favorite game?

A: Super Smash Bros

Q: What do you call one of Mei's jokes?

A: A-mei-zing

Q: What would Pharah say as a weatherwoman?

A: Cloudy with a chance of justice.

Q: What's Reaper's favorite job as a hairdresser?

A: He loves to DYE DYE DYE.

A lot of people say bastion looks young but he's really sentries old!

Q: Why did they hire Soldier 76 as chief web designer?

A: Because he gets everyone in his sites.

Q: What's the difference between a good and bad Pharah?

A: Mercy

Q: Why is Mei so easy to talk to?

A: She knows how to break the ice.

Q: Why doesn't Lucio own a better gun?

A: He keeps breaking them down.

Q: Why couldn't Zenyatta capture the flag?

A: He had no balls.

Q: Why couldn't the enemy team defend against two Junkrats?

A: They were two tired.

Q: Why does Pharah have a crush on Roadhog?

A: She was hooked at first sight.

Starcraft Jokes

Q: **How did the marines safely cross a mine field in the dead of night?**

A: It was under a full moon.

Q: **How many Blizzard employees does it take to screw in a lightbulb?**

A: No one knows because they can't even balance the ladder.

Q: What did the Reaper do when the Queen spawned?

A: It terRan.

A marine walked into a bar. There was no counter.

Q: What computer does IdrA use?

A: IBM

Q: Why can't stalkers win staring contests?

A: They always blink.

Q: Why can't hydralisks get girlfriends?

A: Because they turn into lurkers.

Thank you for reading! If you enjoyed the book, leave us a review and let us know what you liked or what you would like to see next.

If you enjoyed the book and got some good laughs, be sure to check out our other joke books by searching "Hayden Fox Jokes" on Amazon!

Manufactured by Amazon.ca
Bolton, ON